A JAR OF MOTHS

A JAR OF MOTHS

Poems

Ilene Millman

RAGGED SKY PRESS

Princeton, New Jersey

Copyright © 2024 by Ilene Millman

Published by Ragged Sky Press
270 Griggs Drive
Princeton, NJ 08540
raggedsky.com

Library of Congress Control Number: 2023951619

All Rights Reserved

ISBN: 978-1-933974-57-6

This book has been composed in Verdigris MVB and Profile

Text and cover design by Pamela L. Schnitter

Cover image courtesy of Shutterstock

Author photo by Miguel Pagliere

Printed on acid-free paper. ∞

Printed in the United States of America

Contents

When it's over, I want to say: all my life
I was a bride married to amazement.
—MARY OLIVER

for Marty, my husband of 58 years
then, now, always my love, my best friend

for my grandchildren: Aryeh, Binny, Mordechai,
Meir, Shlomo, Audrey, Amanda, Maya, and Sasha

ONE

TO MY BROOKLYN ACCENT

It was easy to identify me then. A *Noo Yawka*.
Your distinctive vernacular, heavy
on the ear, marked me,
the ways I pronounced consonants
or didn't
and though my father's *dem*, *dose* and *dese*
had never flowered
my r's disappeared or appeared
in predictable places.
    I *nevah* minded you or could tell you *apaht* 'til college
    when, *bumma*, you and *ya* great *idears* shoved me
    right inta Speech 101
where they told me you were low-class
uneducated, crude
where they mocked your vowels,
said you pulled them apart like saltwater taffy
and stuffed them into words
turning *sausage* into *sawww-sidge*,
where they laughed at your *LongGuyland*
and showed me by every action the need
to rid myself of that other within me.

This morning I looked up at old photos
perched on the shelf above my desk.
I listen hard to find you in the shape
of my mother's voice
    Take yah sistah and go play. Heah. Catch.
I see a skate key wrapped in a tissue
plummet from an open fourth floor window
We were together then.
I listen. I hear
your rhythms and curious inflections
your music, so long gone.

KINTSUGI

The old teacup once belonged to my mother—
iridescent-gold ceramic, prismatic hues
like a hidden pearl on the inside, Czech-made.

It was a rush-and-tumble morning—
I was doing diligence
dusting china cabinets,

a momentary incandescent curve
and shards
splatter the kitchen floor.

The Japanese restore such things
with precious metal,
the seams highlighted,

maybe they're the point after all—
the random pattern of shatter, like wounds
leaving different marks on each of us.

Now, when I stare off into gargoyled darkness
at four in the morning
running from something I said

or did—some fear, or some insistence of the past
under the floor of everything, can I have some love
for the shatter and seams of my life,

blame less the ways I've broken
and convince myself
each of these scars is precious?

TO MY BODY

You're so   clingy.
Always glomming onto me
like moss on a stone
since the day I was born—
worse than my shadow who at least
has the decency to disappear for a few hours.
You smell if I don't wash you.
You need to be kept warm
or you quake and rattle,
but not too warm or you leak.
You guzzle chocolate, add pounds.
Picking and poking my gut with those knives
you carry, you interrupt
my sleep. And lately
you're more expensive
to maintain, your belts and hoses
need repair or replacement.
Without you everything would be easy,
free
from sleeping, breathing—
no belly, no arthritic knees,
no high cholesterol, no cholesterol at all.
If I could just get you off
my back for a few hours,
put you on loan to Body Worlds,
I'd go off to Siesta Beach
without an umbrella, without
a hat, without sunscreen
I'd go even further
to a mountaintop in Tibet,
to the rainforest in Brazil,

no baggage
not even a carry-on.
Look, I know in the end
you and I will come to judgment
and you will betray me.
One way or another everyone gets left
but what I need to ask you,
what I'm asking myself,
when you vanish forever into the cold
earth or fire,
will you be transformed,
will I?

RELIC

Counterfeits abound:
holy nails, holy thorns,
fragments of wood invented
from air
but what the Bible first names holy
is no object
but time
holy is a day
its beginnings
and loose ends.

We humans are in constant motion
but unlike a planet or a pendulum
ours is wild, wanton,
incorrigible doing,
the compulsion to stand
before falling down
and shoveling up
the dark throat

but what if after all,
this solitary circulation I call body,
this relic
venerated with every superstition
is irrelevant
and after all this
hanging onto to it

like a helium balloon
untied from around a wrist

a me I never knew was
floats up inside time
smelling sweetly
of good air after rain.

HOW TO BE A TREE

Am I not partly leaves and vegetable mould myself?
—Henry David Thoreau

Never flit
    fly or slip away in the night   Hold still and travel
                                        everywhere
      But be right there
for second looks, for re-
    visiting often   Start off in the dirt
                      of a hillside
                                  on an incline everything
                                      looks possible

From a seed grow
      a trunk with sleeves
            of branches
                            Spread green arcs of leaves
                              Decree the form:
                                  hairy, heart-shaped

saw-toothed like
      the chestnut
                         Decide
                           if you will drop them

      Verse yourself in bird
           if you ask them
           they will teach you

           Sway in the slur of rain
           and bathe in
           liquid mornings

           Converse with soil
           and with sunlight
           replay wind's gossip

           Root around for the
         underground forest web
           find the others

           Every autumn
           light yourself
           in ember-orange

Then watch winter drag her hemline across the mud   jewels of ice flashing
                        from your arms
    Your great clock is slow   Fall in love with the time on your hands.

How is it

when I least expect it
a tripwire flares
wordless—

a curl of *Jean Naté* in a department store

drenches the air with my mother's signature
as much breath as scent—
flirtatious   a clarion

that announces her arrival
and lingers
long after she's gone—

on riffles of spring grasswind

our son after soccer practice—
a pungent funk of boysweat
and something undefinable   tangy—

how is it   like land mines
beneath weedy masses of years
smell detonates memory

a step through any hospital doorway—

the ICU's inarticulate perfume
top notes of alcohol   ammonia
bass note of fear—

air that has pores breathing me in—
scent I can taste
rotten with possibility

how is it   a potent wizard
conjures up summer nights in Brooklyn
from the ether of this oniony pot roast—

assembly line of neighbors
perched on chairs in front
of our old apartment building

garlic, paprika, cinnamon
and burnt rings of Marlboros, Kents
on a dozen tongues

how is   this whelm of aroma reassembles—
an instant standing in—
still burning.

HOW TO TALK WITH US

Don't mention the grief
that came in waves,
the sudden apprehensions
or tightness in the throat—
the need to sigh.

Don't bore us with seances,
we prefer your bedside
just before the lattice
light of morning
and forget about mediums—
we never talk to strangers.

Tell us a good joke.
　　　　Will glass coffins be a success?
　　　　Remains to be seen.
We enjoy a laugh
though it often comes out
more a moan.

Sieve our stories up
from the river
of memory, open rooms
you recognize, big windows full of detail,
love's happiness, love's pain—
it's better not to flinch.

We'll speak to you
through you, the way the sun sparkles
through a fragment of broken glass.
　　　　I'll tell—how I sat so still in the easy chair

    while your children stuck playing cards
    behind my glasses
    and I'll tell—how I stroked your hair
    until you felt safe

And don't forget
say our names out loud
Ida, Rose, Seymour, Ann.

LEGACY

I was imprinted on my father
like a good little gosling
although he was not
the first human I saw.
When I was old enough,
I sometimes waddled after him
to his one-man print shop.
I watched his focus as he set type,
single letter at a time fitted
into the face of the press—
          he made words with his hands
          then spread ink across the metal plate
but from its first downward stroke
I knew he'd flown
far off in the space of elsewhere

the rumble of internal machinery
shuddering with his wondering,
radio talk shows fueled him—
citizen journalists, random people calling in,
political volleyball—
gulping and palpating words
he rose higher than the breath
flowing from himself
and from the heights he inked
interrogatives big and small
          whyness, and why*not*ness
          into the pores of my skin
I saw how wings worked,
his updrafts lifting me.

MEMOIR

My mother was a bird,
not your drab, brown plumage
sit-on-the-nest variety

no, closer to a hummingbird—
when light glinted off her feathers
it bounced, shimmered iridescent

and she could see
the non-spectral ultraviolets
in each of us, even when we did not.

Oh, and could she ever hover,
enforcing caution
and safety in her territory.

I sometimes believed she was an owl—
she saw a hand in a cookie jar,
a cigarette puffing out a window,

her offspring scurrying behind her
back—all, while scrambling eggs or perched
on a green kitchen chair.

Once we were a bit older, she transformed
into a hawk, riding the upper thermals
of our three-story home,

high plaintive whistle
meant for our boyfriends' ears
SEEyouSEEyouSEEyou, Go home.

But I think sometimes she wanted to be a pink-
footed goose—without relying on tailwinds
soaring high above the Himalayas.

CERTAIN ABSENCES AND INTENSITIES

When you were a child
I was the place you anchored—
the plain text of our hearts,
a first-grade Dick and Jane:
Look and See
kids, mother, father,
work and play.

Feeling this life of yours
press in, demanding to be heard—
what did it cost you to travel away
from where you came from?
How much did it hurt
to fly through a wormhole
at the speed of light—
tumble out in your future?

Some of the territory familiar
as Honey Lake—
each time we went there you knew
you'd fish for sunnies,
float on an inner tube,
climb up into the treehouse,
but some of the territory
wilder now: new time zone, language,
goals—map on map—
guides good for only so much.

Your grown-up story's a tightrope
steel-hitched to my belly at one end
and thrown out over another world—

a story we struggle to read—
to decipher letters mirrored
and reversed.
We trace new words with our fingers
one letter at a time.
Sometimes that's all
we can manage.

FINDERS KEEPERS?

Of course, people lose things—
Elizabeth Bishop nailed the art.
It's the finding that
lapses into silence.

Maybe you remember, late one night
our old brown station wagon,
crawling south, I-95 to Charleston—
stopping at the Golden Arches,
you and your sister, a pair of fillies
loping for the john.

Out you came, cloaked
in secret-y giggles,
sequin-sparkly purse in hand,
found on a stall hook,
pink lipstick, bit of cash in
singles, some fives, riches
to a six and nine-year old. No ID.

Maybe you remember, you asked me
What should we do? There's no one in there.
And no one seated at the tables.
I had time for many thoughts
as we sat biting the heads off
the Captain Crook cookies.

Let's give it to the store manager,
the purse and your names, our phone number.
He'll call if someone does or doesn't.

No one dared question
this instinct—we all knew goodness
but as we walked in silence to the car,
your hands stuffed in pockets emptied
of promise, maybe you remember
you whispered to your sister
the lesson learned
If you find something good,
don't tell Mom.

INVITATION TO MY UNBORN CHILD

You there, floating naked
beneath my skin
in the stillness of this late-night hour,
feel my hand stroke

your fluttering foot,
rippling hiccup,
your poking elbow.

Come now, fall headfirst
down the long darkness,
crown and limbs

yes, you have much to remember and learn,
impending dangers,
but such surprises at the end

yes, a shock of cold, pressing its finger
to your skin like a sudden sea breeze
through an opened curtain

but then, there the air,
the sweet scent of milk
and my heart sounds, how familiar.

You are a dream moon in the night
moon. Loop its light around your waist,
now come.

DYSNOMIA

a difficulty or inability to retrieve the correct word from memory

I used to be a linguistic cowboy—
  tight loop of rope
   thrown precisely
around the target
    and yanked toward me
  from the spaces
between synapses—
    nanosecond or two
  and a word was lassoed,
    tied
  but now
   my tongue stumbles
in uncharted terrain—

words wander

  like meandering herds at dusk

    refusing to be called in

  or trampling the gates

   and tangling up in lexical chaos.

  In gaps and fractures

   words play hide and seek

  scattering just beyond my tongue.

Snatched by this stealthy thief,

 will my thoughts exist

if I haven't words to name them?

THAT GARDEN?

Ours was the place for throwaway plants,
the young ones that arrived bruised
with acronym-stained labels
fat with description:
> this one's an unruly weed, upsets the neat rows
> (he has ADHD)
> this one's spindly, unlike our typical variety
> (she's language delayed)
> late bloomer, way too late (he's dyslexic)
> will never bloom, don't think you can save them.
I was a gardener there for 35 years
propping up plants with consonants and vowels,
mostly just vowels, soft short sounds
a, e, i, o, u
like whispers brought close to those who are hoping.
The plants grew slowly
sometimes shrinking back for a season.
> *Isn't it really hard work*, people often asked
> and I found myself saying
> Oh, I don't know, I really like it.
> And just sometimes I'd add
chances are, you've never heard of *Selenicereus*,
that cactus group: ropy looking, covered with spines
stringy and frayed aerial roots grasping.
No one sings its praises,
extols its unique botany, the shape of its spikes
the functioning of its root system
but when it blooms
late to be sure
the flower is immense, a full foot across.
We have those.

MEDITATION

I have need of ocean's blue acres
gliding past granite gates,
clots of white clouds weightless in their spaces

and I have need of constellations
stomping in their celestial stalls,
yellow wildflowers galloping across a field.

I have need of the pomegranate sour
that is also sweet, like a trombone slide
suspended in night air,

and I have need of the burble
babble and belly laugh of children,
the bouquet of their skin after baths.

I have need of memories
littered with heritable traits,
home-time faces and soft mouths

echoing names: Anne, Cy, Rose,
their braided voices residual
like the ocean in a shell.

I have need of others elbowing
into my heart, piled in on each other,
there's always room

and I have need of the unexpected
escaping jars colored like dreams
or nightmares inching me into other selves,

and look, right here in the center
where everything can happen,
I have need of you, Love.

Oh yes, I have need of you,
the beating resonance of our bodies
fingers on the one drumskin.

FOR MY LOVE ON HIS 80TH BIRTHDAY

let us not repeat the lies
told by numbers,
make jokes about forgetting words
or say if our faces slip
in the fogged bathroom mirror,
if we can touch our toes quick
and supple like a robin landing

let us not make mention
of how things have come untied
like shoelaces
or what we used to be good at
and now are no good at all

let us not hammer at
how quickly noon became night
or what's whispered to us at 2 AM:
what we've done and left
undone, mortal boundaries
or the possible natures of time

instead let's do this:
say aloud a moment larger now
like how it is when we glide
in on our bikes, the beautiful miles
traveled yet again

or the other day,
walking in the Gardens
and seeing those Twilight Zone roses
pulsing off their stems,

fruity purple growing
louder and louder

or just now
when I whispered
I'll always love you
three times in a row,
not the words meandered and multiplied
but the low untranslatable song
of things folded between us
and our laughter
like the sound of many rivers

SKYPING WITH MY GRANDSON WHO
LIVES IN ISRAEL

I performed our vowels
and consonants
my voice chocolate chip cookies.
        You danced the very same vowels and consonants
        your toes tap tapping
        rhythms unfamiliar to me.

Maybe a little slower? I say.
Maybe a little clearer? You say.

As for what we do not grasp
let it baffle beneath the fig tree.
As for the signals of our hearts
        let's braid them like olive-green vines
        across this visible expanse
        and hum together, *we.*

While reading the travel catalog

I decide I do need a vacation,
a vacation from the fulcrum
of my heart rhythms, sometimes rocking
160 beats-a-minute like Jerry Lee
pounding *Great Balls of Fire*
and sometimes Johnny crooning *Chances Are.*

What I need is an ocean cruise,
exotic ports, no repacking my clothes,
all the stuff I lug around muffled in a carry-on,
the obligations
of the wool toes of socks.

I need a slow cruise and a land excursion
far away from the anxiety tributaries
of my children's lives dotted with troubles
cropping up again and again like rogue weeds
in sylvan glades

and I need an Arctic getaway
from the daily news, what someone wants hidden
and someone else wants stomped
with the delicacy of a black rhino
battering through the bush.

There in the small print,
still available, a hammock sized for two
swinging in the day's ordinary breath,
where my lips can graze the salt of your shoulder,
new grass flaring fervent green.

TRANSFORMATION

Even as a four-year old
you had fine-boned
delicate fingers reaching out
for names—
a round-faced boy
tapping a world flapping
about in books.
Look, grandma, the caterpillar's in the pupa.
And look now, a butterfly.

Later, you taught me about lacuna: the hole in the story.
The caterpillar finds a quiet place, attaches
a pupa. Inside there, it doesn't sprout delicate wings from furry body
like a tadpole grows legs—it liquefies. From protein and fiber mush—
a completely different creature.

Embossed with name and body—
you too did not simply grow wings
and this part of the story is missing still.
There are no directions
for leaving childhood.
Something liquefies perhaps—
a bright life flows around a single heart
and takes shape—
a solace of soft tissue
nothing as it was.
What flutters
into the vanishing point
of the future
a wholly different creature.

CLEPSYDRA

an ancient time-measuring device worked by the flow of water

A vast scaffold
across our world
lays down laws of time
    equal
        a second is a second,
    you can count them
        absolute, predictable, Divine even
but now
after my many days, decades
now my time moves more
    like a water clock
        liquid flowing,
    dripping into a catch-bowl
        and only in the bowl do I see the lines

see how much time has passed
to determine what rites
and sacrifices to perform
    and the water flow speeds up
        or slows now with the temperature
    and humidity of the evening news,
        a phone call from my son, a poem.

I ask myself why I even need to know
the time of day now,
only the mind moving through itself

how could it possibly matter
            and why do I turn
       my wrist to check the minutes
              except maybe to remind myself
to tend them
to count them and to tend them.

FACES IN THE MIRROR

if God were a woman
would daughters have free will?

>   the free will of daughters
>   to slough off a mother

shake free of the mother
and come to light glorious in self

>   in the time the mother comes into light
>   dragging her longing, unmet hope

her longing hope for an Eden sealed off at the exits.
I will have to follow my daughters

>   I will have to follow their glorious selves
>   fly off to get on with it

fly off from unity once desired, always imperfect
mother, daughter, woman, God.

PHONE HOME

A phone is like a jar of moths—
a jar of moths set deep inside your chest.
The disruption of a *Ring, Ring*
ruptures your sleep   or your meal
or your heart's tick
and when you answer
the lid lifts   and the moths
flutter out in a flash of wings.

I'll never be loved again.
I'll die a cold flounder
on a barren ocean floor
moans my teenage daughter—
                at midnight—
        from her freshman dorm—
in Delaware   128.5 miles away

and the pitch-roil flutter of moths
carries her pain into my mind
where it becomes   everything
and entirely mine.

She hiccups a farewell into my ear
where I keep her voice   her pauses
where I don't name them anything   but her.
I hear *Click*. Dead air.
In perfect darkness and perfect silence
the moths eat through my woolly night hours
while the phone
                sits flat-bottomed   and so quiet
            on the nightstand beside my bed.

A CONVERSATION WITH GOD

after the painting The Jewish Angel *by Giorgio de Chirico*

You never make it easy, do You?

This Jewish angel,
carrying Your message I suppose
but no injunction to believe.
So why not a spotted pink curve
to wrestle with the angles?

What I'm looking for still, meaning
firm as if crafted from metal, gongs
like a bell clapper in a windstorm
though I'd settle for dreams
with round edges

but what You've sent me so far—
wingless shape,
a heart space
inchoate
like an oversize eye,

a face I cannot see.

MYSTICAL MUD

lately I've been wondering about
unknowable things
              is there a God
and what does she want from us
and what does it mean
the burning bushes, faces in potato chips
or the long intervals where nothing is heard?

Why in a universe of random chaos
do we expect fairness
              and did Adam have a bellybutton?
Should I be ready to accept
what I don't hear or see
but only suspect might
      or might not

and then in today's news
mysterious mud
        gooey, viscous, gelatinous muck,
hauled from some secret spot
along a New Jersey riverbank
by an old guy with a gray ponytail
this stuff singular

in its ability to de-slippify baseballs,
a muddy miracle blessing every major league ball
        rule 4.01 of umpire duties, solemn and Talmudic—
how mud smeared on a handmade five-ounce sphere
held together with 108 red stitches
        makes it possible for a human
to hurl it 100 miles an hour toward another human

SHOE SHOPPING WITH EMILY D

not quite a cento

Time collapses the picture—so I can see you here—slim as a year
and quietly strolling the DSW aisles—high-button shoes delicate
as birds beneath your white dress not out of place in these aisles—
I confess I want to be seen with you in public—I have knocked
upon your door and now I want to keep your key and give you
mine—I want to go shopping with you Emily D

let's roam this thicket of detail—knowing meaning can be lost in
the facts—these are called wedges and chunky-heeled pumps, and
open-toed sandals letting pleasure through—let's link arms now
and pretend we're nobody—the pair of us

strolling past the sneakers—I can see upon what falls your eye—
upon what your smile—that pair of orange and chartreuse run-
ning shoes—Yes they would surely fit your windy feet—stooping
to secure them I blink and you are gone—swift as a bird that flies
away—inebriate of air—twigs of story in her beak.

INSIDE, OUTSIDE, UPSIDE-DOWN

Because this old house is the shell—
the non-I riding shotgun for the I—
a shelter of palpable shadow
that settles and sighs around me.
Because in that space
the space of me lies in a cradle
of nooks and crannies.

Because there one day
I'm swinging a duster
left right left like a metronome
across the desk in the now gray study,
its floor strewn with uneaten words
and suddenly, I squint my eyes, see
the old playroom there—

the circus print on the wall,
that raucous ride of upside-down—
and smell the fragrance
of sleepy smallness,
hear high-pitched light spark
the now-quiet to toddler giggles.

Yesterday, reports from Hawaii:
towers of flame, faces of blaze,
the newsman in the ash-stippled shirt pointing
to piles of rubble—
because then they spoke of recovery—
of when, but not of how—
and I wondered

would sorrow for a fallen house fill
the universe forever after
or after
the roiling fury, would some carapace
of me set itself on the ground
inside out like a nest in a field
on the threshold of new being

PEACE

The morning sun is sharp.
Between the woods' woven shadows
I step around puddles,
gold light dabbling
the water, the unseen listening
to my mind's mumblings.
Isn't there always
something listening?

My ear grows accustomed
to wider and wider intervals
between the four-stroke
of car engines, voices,
the still stations blooming
under sun-spattered leaves
and I remember

the quiet-flooded hours last night,
rain thick as glass
and I lay with you, curled
in the curve of your body,
your marrow in my bones,
my pulse in your fingertips,
our breath and the rain the only thrum.

IN PRAISE OF UNDERLINED AND DOG-EARED PAGES

As a child I never once transgressed, never violated
your 11th commandment, Mom: *Thou shalt not deface books*
and never a library book

I'm not sure just when my vandalism began—
those folds in upper corners of pages, pencil tracings,
me prattling to myself in the margins

but now I pick up my old books, not for the long reread
but just for dog-ears and underlines,
echoes of some prior version of me, totally taken

with the Nauset tribes on Cape Cod
digging ceremonial sand holes to record
important events (page 79, Dillard, *Maytrees*)

hidden in the folds of a fallen tree
groups of ladybugs
called a *loveliness* (page 105, Renkl, *Late Migrations*)

and *once my nose crawled like a snail on the glass*
(in an old poetry anthology, page 266, Lowell,
The Union Dead)

who I was when I read the page
and thought to save it
converses with the who I am now

here and here again,
saving different lines,
happy for the haunting.

TWO

IN PRAISE OF RANDOM THINGS, JUNE 21ST

Praise for the light—its certainty, the way it fractures
into geometric patterns I see tracing
on the sidewalk, the way it clings to the wings of birds.

Praise for Zoom—the way the early morning visit
with my grandson sketches missing pieces in my family portrait
like stick figures trying their best to become real.

For the waffle sandwich—gobs of blueberries and strawberries
stuffed between two Belgians and topped with more whipped
cream than the Himalayas have snow.

For the house wren riot—and the way the ruby-throated packet of
hyper-caffeinated energy sipped my sugar syrup for 6 nanoseconds
before flitting away.

Blessing for little blonde boy—holding his nylon shorts away
from his sides like a blue sail lifting
in the wind, running and laughing the whole way down my block.

Rise up in praise for the Amazon rep—who did not disconnect me,
disrespect me, disapprove
or disappoint me.

Praise for Wordle—in two moves

For chord progressions—the skeletons of songs rattling
their twelve-bar bluesy bones in my AirPods,
accompaniment for my walking pulse

And the lone doe—the way she tiptoes in the whisper music
of grass just at dusk and delicately nibbles
my neighbor's fallen fruit instead of my flowers and shrubs.

Praise for your good-night kiss—4 hugs in held suspension, books
on my night table, the entirety of them, bread dough
that did not fail to rise, 60 ounces of water, indoor plumbing

This good hair day—dark chocolate and coffee, coffee and dark
chocolate, for the completely possible poem,
the smile on my friend's face when we met for lunch

For the chipmunk so quick I did not run it over—and the light,
the way the lemon bash of it
drops at day's end like a scene change in the theater.

SCRAPED CLEAN IN ISTANBUL

All dusty day shopping
she wants a spa
        hygienic   modern
and I   want an epic
        Cagaloglu Hammam Turkish Baths   den of indulgence

   no haggling here   we pay and plunge
        into a domed room   marble fountain center stage,
through high eyelet windows   slitted light white as paper.
First   the getting bare
        not as difficult as it once was
old bodies unnoticed like old people.
        We slip into place
  on a communal marble slab.
We wait.   Sweating.   Naked.

In comes a Turkish warrior   disguised
        as a woman
packed in a bathing suit
        and speaking not a lick
        of English

massaged
mashed
muscles   leg to head
  tremble beneath her hands   like a horse
        quivers beneath its rider,
she starts again
  her hand now covered with a coarse cloth mitt
        scrubbing   scraping   raking—

the years slough off   lie on the tile floor
        and then a deluge of doubled soapsuds
           over our heads.

An hour gone in flying particles
bodies vibrating like the aftertone of a struck tuning fork,
        our hair frazzled frizz
    our eyes raccooned   by runaway mascara
she smiles   had we never realized how beautiful we are?

CLOUDY WITH A CHANCE OF HYPERBOLE

Bomb cyclone coming
pronounces the weather anchor—
ARkStorm, a thousand-year event
asserts his counter-
part pointing
to the flashy contour map—

See, there's a series of atmospheric rivers,
some of the Pineapple Express variety
along the Pacific
and a polar vortex in the north.
Competing colors, graphics
runaway verbiage

but of course, last spring
where I live, school closures announced
one Tuesday night—tropical storm,
lightening lashed skies, epic rains,
floods forecast, millions in damage—
not quite
a thimbleful dappled my pink azaleas.

Isn't that the problem with weather—
like an 18-wheeler wrapped in rags of mist
barreling down the highway
ghost-gray contours 'til it screams past
barely raising a hair on your head
or hitting you like
well, like a truck.

Forever prey to certitude
I heed the words of prophets

hovering over crystal
barometer, thermometer
anemometer, hygrometer
but stash a blue sunhat
and a polka-dot umbrella
under the front seat of my car
certainty: possible.

LAUGHING WOMAN

after "Hidden Smile," a photograph by Réhahn, 2011

A labyrinth of detail written in the wrinkles,
the marks on the hands,
isn't the body a map of where it has been,
but like a single soft breath
this purple-pigmented patch of joy,
the momentary duration
of this one inexplicable moment
fleet and fleeing,
you caught it by its translucent wing,
you know it won't stop
the sun's wild wheel
so you hold onto it,
fingertips to forehead and mouth,
you make a frame for your eyes to see
this frangible dazzle
aloft in the rare air of time
so like the throb of a star
humming its own secret present tense.

EDWARD'S MUSE

after Morning Sun, *Edward Hopper, 1952. Jo Hopper modeled for
all the female figures in her husband's paintings between 1924 and
his death in 1957.*

slants of light
    reveal   conceal
  secrets and rumors
        hanging   in the same reflection

I look alone   seated on a bed
    knees pulled up
  to my chest

glancing lapis sky
    window open   for the wind to leave
        no border
      between body and imagination

practiced in the art   of creating
    still-life
  morning sun   mirrors his interior

  light long-shadows the bed
    illuminates the wall beside me
like an empty thought

my ever-present voyeur
  only watching
  through the window
  of his palette

DRIVING IN PORTUGAL

Here spring slips in quickly—
rising from deep winter lethargy
birds carry the sun skyward
and mountains shrug off
a shawl of white.
Here I learn about shoulders:
steep drop-offs, sheer rock walls
of schist, and everywhere
terraces dropping
into the valley—
earth-filled stone shelf
atop stone shelf balanced
like acrobats—
the grapevines stand black shoulder
to black shoulder,
tufts of leaves like green epaulets.
The sense of river and old trees
envelops me.
We stop at a wall encircling Evora
where again I learn
about shoulders: the Neoliths
then the Visigoths,
the Romans, the Moors 900 years,
the Christians
each straddling then destroying
what stood before,
who leaves a trace—
a megalith, an aqueduct,
a fragmented wall
its knees stained green.
But even traces sing.
I hear them in the language

in cowbells, in the water
that folds over the bows
of riverboats on the Douro
and I smell traces
in the wild roses, wisteria—
see them in the spindly green shoots
on shoulders of grapevines.

LOSING THE NINTH

Sfyria is a language of whistles spoken by only 18 people in the world on the small Greek Island of Evia

The symphony in my head never makes it to the page.
Consonance is missing: the mannequin fails
to wear its lyrical clothes,
violins come in late,
cello off-key, movement too slow
or too fast. Conversation drowns
in garbled grammar while I wave my pencil baton
afraid to lose
ability to write with capital letters.
Perhaps it is true: poetry is only
an elegant way of screaming.
Tone-deaf form slinks away,
words fold on themselves, mere avatar.
Still, I find myself unspooling
like a blank tape hiss, like a dial tone
buzzing from my electronic heart—
there must be something there sleeping in the creases—
some sound to capture the fingerprint of breath,
calling out who and what and why.
A train whistle steam-trumpets from a mile away
into night air and through my open window,
its six-chambered bell cast into a single sound.
It's then I think about the village of Antia
amid giant Cycloptic boulders
where the world is named,
ordered, collected in a whistle.

RUBY-RED CHERRY WOO

Before the wig and the hoop skirt
before whalebone corsets
pleats, drapes and shoulder straps
there was lipstick.

Carmine red hyperbole and heat
squeezed from cochineal insects
boiled in ammonia—

a tender yield—
vivid red drops
to form a Cupid's Bow.

Some say lipstick killed her—
Queen Elizabeth that is—
half inch of lead-laden
pop of color on her dead lips.

What was here before, still here.
Isn't that us looking, relying
on others to see us

and aren't we still willing
to put almost anything on our lips
for a picture-perfect pout.

Every morning, sitting at my vanity
I apply my face loosely
with just the right amount
of carelessness

lips pencil-outlined
then swipe, vampy red or pale pink
the pearlescence of my lipstick
made from shimmery scales of fish—
mostly herring

QUIETUDE

"There are only, at most, 12 places left in the U.S. where one can go without hearing any human caused noise." —Gordon Hempton

There is little Quiet in the world.
Even as we are brought forth with noise:
beings raucous as we are mortal.

Even as myths of creation are sonic:
Boom, Babble, Brouhaha.
And God said, *Let there be…*

The city drowns me in sound:
thick traffic, thin walls,
outside   endless engines thrust, combust,

inside   noises made with faucets, pans,
cellphone squawk, computer hum,
refrigerator thrum, relentless

pandemonium.

Some linguists say the oldest word
is hist = listen:
to cicadas who burst

into song at birth, to drops of rain
belling off cedar bough,
grass-wind, pine-wind hymn—

a sonic pulse like a fugue
moves through a world that won't
stop talking.

ON A FLAGSTONE PATH

Rudolf W. van der Goot Rose Garden, Somerset, New Jersey

From the lily pond just ahead I hear the brown bullfrog,
his mournful yet eager sound like the creaking of a door.
Overhead, rippled birdvoice flaps
into the rustle and rub of bushes.
Before, behind, beside   an eruption of color:
rose brigades bulging pink, purple, red,
each one overspills its name: Lavender Veranda,
Red Cascade, City of New York.
I bend over to catch a close-up
of yellow bee gossip,
of tender tints in their increase and diminishing.
Bud, blossom   then the small round fruit,
the sweet-tart flavor
of life gone past its bloom.

RITA'S POND

The bullfrog choral line,
melody composed from pondsunk plants
from mud and dark and sun,
a green symphony
of parts and desires
it swells and fades, rinses the air
those faint wakes of what
mud and dark and sun
birth down at the pond bottom
while time turns slowly silken
and I keep still and listen and wonder
when we each of us are gone
under, does some part or desire
emerge as song?

PAPER HOUSE

built by Elis F. Stenman, Rockport, Massachusetts, 1924

He was curious—
wanted to see
what would happen
to the paper.

Isn't this what we humans do?
We want to know.
We want to build
a heart
out of what we have
in front of us
despite the threat
of fire   rain.

Recipe for paper walls:
Ingredients; 100,000 newspapers, flour, water, apple peels, varnish.
Preparation: Combine in small batches: flour, water, & apple peels.
Stir until thickened into paste. Place a page, headlines-up on a flat
surface. Smear a dollop of paste & spread. Pancake stack the next
layer of newspaper & baste with paste, careful not to lean it left or
right. Repeat 215 times. Tuck in deckled edges & press to squeeze
out the noise. Frost layers with varnish, leaving words readable:
Maine...antique...moment. Serve up these panels & install.

He lived here ten summers
made the furniture too
from paper logs he rolled—
front pages exposed.

On a dining chair we read
Lindbergh Hops Off for Ocean Flight to Paris;

on a grandfather clock the mastheads of city newspapers;
on a radio cabinet, Hoover's presidential campaign—
a rattling baffle and a thing
becomes another—
the past's presence in the present. Maybe

this is the best we can do—
pry the heart
from the center of the world,
all the newspapers, the passports, receipts
permits, blueprints—
roll them up into a chair.

LUNCH ATOP A SKYSCRAPER

after a NY Herald Tribune *photograph, October 2, 1932. Anonymous*

If you look without looking—
eleven ironworkers lunch on a suspended I-beam
legs dangling 850 feet above midtown Manhattan,
the vastness of Central Park behind
urban abyss below.

Bookended, one guy lights a cigarette,
the other glares at the camera,
immigrant aspiration and determination
summarized in their casual recklessness.
Actually—

in the art creating this still-life, insider traders
divert the eye away from the beam, a steel beam
suspended just a few feet above the finished 69th floor
of the RCA building, the photo staged
to sell real estate

and at the very periphery, steel production's
dirty business: opencast mining, greenhouse gases,
water contaminants, solid wastes, toxic air pollution.
The casual recklessness of Earth's embezzlers,
their endless aspiration.

COMING TO AMERICA

after a photograph by Lewis W. Hine, 1926

Not for the proportion
or symmetry recognized as beauty
but shadows, the fine facial lines
that hold onto every feeling,
the soft body of need
folded more tightly than blanket corners
and your resolve, it also matters.
We never spoke of practical nightmares
not how you changed but how things do,
how you can stand firmly planted in a hurricane
of events, but only in the eye,
how you can wrap your past tense
in a heavy woolen scarf
fling it out over a molten sea.

MOUNTAIN MELODY

If it weren't for the rocks in its bed, the stream would have no song
—Carl Perkins, American singer songwriter

I dig my fingertips into earth's crumbling geography
picking up pink pebbles along this Maine beach,
nothing whole,
the split and burr of fragment.

Only softness is vulnerable we think
but mountains heave to their own necessity
the rocks moved and broken down.

A fragment, by definition a thing imperfect
diminished by having less.

Remnants of the last blood-orange stains of sunset
clinging to the horizon
I spot a gray stone half-buried in shallows
heart shaped when I lift it out

dark line running through,
all its edges smoothed out.
This fractal grain of mountain has heard

the crack, felt the broken
sum of things.

I rub it between my fingers,
listen for wind-song,
river-song

an oncoming beating heart.

IMMIGRANT

How does a boy
keep still through the long anticipation
bouncing 500 miles, Tijuana to California,
in the dark arms of need
in a crate of darkness
fastened to the bottom of a truck?

How does a boy,
face of peach-fuzz and journey pride
wait, hope unbandaged
like a wound,
pilgrim eyes on a glimpse
of who he might become?

How does a boy?

He's from somewhere else.
Isn't everyone though?
Traveling from where roads begin,
dreaming with his heart
outstretched as if it were a hand,
shoes covered with dust.

THE OCTOPUS ESCAPES

In dextral spiral of blue pulse,
haptic down aquarium halls and down a drain,
his single jumpy heart, a nucleus of flight.

Haptic down aquarium halls, and down a drain
his eight limbs cup the world in incandescent curve.
As he tastes the edge of ocean

his eight limbs cup the world in incandescent curve
and skip of the wrist, he vanishes,
his single jumpy heart a nucleus of flight.

And skip of the wrist, he vanishes
in dextral spiral of blue pulse
as he tastes the edge of ocean.

The first time we saw a hummingbird in our yard

a sound like a hyper-caffeinated bumblebee, a black shadow
propelled by high-octane fuel

took time
out from our mundane moment

left us dumb,
this smallest packet

of metallic green energy
flitting and flinging air

then hovering, posing
just outside our window

like a sequined beauty queen,
eyes staring through the glass, ours, his.

Like an idea, an inspiration that appears
uncatchable and vanishes when it wants.

With all our human sway and swagger
we can't command an encore

like happiness we can only grab
when it rushes by

flashing its bright green feathers.

HOW BAKING BREAD CAN SAVE YOU

Imagine yourself,
floury apron, centering a golden-brown
loaf on grandma's rose platter.
Then stop looking and feel.
You see, what you see first
is a shaggy, lumpy mess—flour, water, yeast

but plunge your hands in. Wet. Tacky.
Focus on the fall of your shoulders,
on your fingers,
strands of dough hanging off
each one like butterfly clusters above
damp leaves.
Now watch how you press-stretch-press
with the heel of your hand

quarter turn
press again, folding the dough
over on itself, letting the air in.
Notice how far you can stretch
in a new direction,
minutes ago, it was nothing.

At first the dough springs back
like wrestling with an octopus
or an angel
but remember it's an aria
for your hands.

Consider the whens. When is enough.
When to stop

pushing, always the question.
Then wait for this thing
made of ambition
to rise,
like the sun, like flying, like magic.

Pace-peek, vacuum-peek, phone-call peek,
the secret holds itself fast
the suspense eternal.

THREE

These unforeseen times rather—

after Gerard Manley Hopkins

we could name them unknowable
and unknowable call them uncertain
as in uncertain is unstable.
Unstable is a two-legged chair
in shallow water wobbling
in endless waves of shouting

the water itself unstable
we can't control its shape—
a whisper of water
until it rises
a tsunami.

Each of us a collection
of particles in fluid
motion, we all churn
and like water over a sluice,
each day the winches may jam
the scaffolding collapse—

what to do with such instability?

How do we haul ourselves up
to begin again with a new hurrah—
like dolphins along the long white margin
of the sea, shadowsplash plunge and surface,
lapse but emerge—lapse, emerge

another unforeseen latitude,
air fat and salty.

AFTERMATH

more mass shootings than days in 2023

hailstorms of condolences
pummel our airwaves,
slick and slippery
chunks of words piling up
to astonishing depths,
the deep drifts taking weeks
to melt away
as they always do

some people say
for things like this
there are no words
but what they mean is
some words pulled and stretched
so far left and right
that they are transparent
like thoughts and prayers
and some words riddled
with bullet holes
and poured into
concrete slabs of sorrow
so heavy
we cannot lift them to the page

CRIME SCENE

November 2020

If I were collecting evidence
wouldn't I look at the tire tracks
tracing broken distances
living to dead
in stock dividends and expense accounts—
who has the motive—they who look like citizens
changing the map
leaving no forwarding address?

If I were collecting evidence
wouldn't I analyze photographs,
video recordings, tweets
brittle as promises
and autopsy the bones
cracked like hope
and stacked deep
in boxes of discord?

If I were the one collecting evidence
shouldn't I unpack the fingerprints
floating fibers, strands of hair
from the briefcases of influence
brushing what's there to see
and lay them end to end
across this current carnage—
a measure of the outstretched fingers of God
or the smallest fisted hand?

LILITH GOES TO CONEY ISLAND

I can still picture us   in-your-face red dress covering
        my serpentine body and Judith   lemon yellow miniskirt
vinyl Go-Go boots. Father-God always whispered
                we were a bit brash and seductive—
    maybe that's why He removed her story   edited mine.

Q train to Coney Island   my idea of course—
        didn't think Miriam would come
but she's changed   those years waiting
                for Him to speak through her   then finding
    herself shamed for what   speaking up

I remember how Jephthah's daughter
        danced to Miriam's tambourine that day
the other nameless ones trailing after her   quiet as usual—
                the ones who begat unto   who begat unto who
and the Egyptian princess   the hospitable gentile woman—

and how we didn't even ask Eve to come
        Eve with her *yes dear*   *no thank you dear*—
we left her in that bland paradise
                crocheting yarmulkas   though truth be told
    she was never dumb   or evil.

Fresh off the train   we hit the Cyclone
        I can still feel it   wind rushing through my hair
blood pumping in my veins, yes, no   faster
                don't look, must look   a scream escaping
    hiss of brakes

how I dared them   the Parachute Jump
        the long slow lift   climax on top

release and free fall   Adam would never do this
                  but damn, it had closed down   too much risk
   not enough security

By then we were hungry.
          noses pressed to a candy-store window
they coveted cherry-red candy apples
               so much sweeter than the Garden ones

  Nah,
          I said, *we already know what we need to know*

And how finally claiming ourselves
         we strode up Surf Ave. and up
onto the Boardwalk
           munching salty Nathan's French fries
      before an open sea.

FRACTURED ABECEDARIAN FOR A REFUGEE

February 2022

It's called *armed* conflict when men toting assault rifles face off with
old ladies carrying eggs
Called *bombardment* when your building looks like a broken dollhouse,
furniture open to the sky
A *camp* when it's makeshift tents ringed by barbed-wire fences
and there are no swim lessons
Called *displacement* when you're moved from a town where people
lie dead in the street
Evacuation when they map out the routes then guess how much time
Family when women and children leave husbands and fathers behind
And *genocide* when it's not accidental
It's called a *host* country where they agree to take you in but haven't
finished making the beds
Idiomatic when you don't understand
And *journalism* when someone photographs your despair, saves it
on a flash drive
It's called *Kyiv* where you came from. You took nothing but the children.
It's called *large scale* when missiles light the sky like fireworks, but
no one claps
Mass casualty when your bleeding sister is carried from the hospital
Navigating the upheaval when you use Telegram channels
to find a bed
It's called only a special military *operation* when it isn't
A *question*, if cluster bombs, atomic bomb, thermobaric weapons
Called *pleading* when you elbow your way onto the last train leaving
Repeated exposure when each day dawns dressed as horror

Zeroing out when everything comes to nothing
And it's called *yourself*, what you no longer recognize
It's called *X-tra* when you lug the giant stuffed shark your son hangs
    onto for comfort
Waiting in a quiet panic, your car inching toward a border
By *virtue* of your race when you're shoved off the aid line
And *unending* all the dead ends
It's called *technology* when you instant message the son you haven't
    heard from in three days
And you're called a *survivor* when you've lost everything but your life

FOR MY GRANDSON'S ZOOM BAR MITZVAH

Even tight shoes
one may grow accustomed to—
pressure on some small spot

the soft skin dies
forms a hardened layer. Eventually.
These facts waiting like frogs for a fairy tale

but see, there's this particular pair—
tight, strappy shoes stashed
at the back of my closet—

time spun in transparent loops
across the instep—bonded and sewn
connections—and when I wedge them on,

I hear laughter, like the sound of rivers gurgling.
Bought those shoes
for my sixtieth birthday bash—

wore them for your big brother's bar mitzvah.
Oh, did I mention they're blue
and even though my fancy blouse is blue

and my made-up face zoomed—
particle wave wonder—the 6000 miles
between *u* and *i* in *unconditional*—

to where you stand swaying forward and back—
to where you chant the words you've practiced,
today, my feet are bare.

A YEAR IN

March 11, 2021

A blue funk in sunk in a fly in amber   a pig in a poke.
No walk in the park   this tempest in a teapot. This stitch in time
a brick in my hand   its foot in my door   like a fox in the henhouse.
Plugged in   unhugged in   in what, a year in?
A woman's place in   in the homein inthehome   a man's place inthehome
inthehome the child   cuckoo in the nest.   Sitting in the catbird seat
couched in, down in   drawn in and done in   carved in stone. No exit.

At this juncture/point in time, Oh, to be

out in left field   back in business   full swing in quest of.
Caught in the act of   caught up in   in cahoots with.
To be in contact   incontactwithcontact   in good company
intouch   intouch with   walking out and about in
and in view of.   Knee deep in, teeth in   zhuzhed up, laughing in the aisles.
Out in   all in   in awe of.

ON HEARING MUSIC FOR THE FIRST TIME IN SIX MONTHS

Mozart at Morven, September 13, 2020

I'd been homesick for something
I could not describe   lost joy perhaps
gone unnoticed amid all that bruising
us at the time.

Eleven masked musicians sit cloistered
inside   spaced between propped-open doors,
the two of us slouched outside
on plastic lawn chairs plunked
in uncertain ranks of six-foot squares of grass,
imitate the 4/4 time of normal
life beneath a blue and indifferent sky.

Then, cast like a line catching
connection   first notes summoned from strings,
we watch the swaying listing dipping
of shoulders, the flying of hair, flash of bow,
sound weaves threads of color
and draws up calls and sighs,
melting iced minor keys of fear   of longing.

QUIETUDE REVISITED, 2020

Just twelve places he wrote in 2012—
twelve places in America
where one can stand and hear
no human sound.

Yet today, only a short walk
from my house, a stand of trees,
not a forest by any means
just a path through some woods but there,
now the silence is wide
so wide you can almost hear
the sound of clouds
cruising low above the roofs
stroking the tops of oak and pine.

As I walk, the crunch of my sneakers—
acorns on asphalt like treading over grains of sugar.
No planes, no car engines, no human voice
but the one in my head—
background becomes foreground:
the sound of water running,
my nylon jacket swooshing
as I swing my arms

I stand still, count ten seconds,
twenty, one minute, two—
birdsong rises up from the silence
like soft breath,
interweaves with quiet—
four minutes, five—each moment
newly arrived
open and pink.

So what have you been doing lately?

October 15, 2020

durational performance—
it's an art form—*waiting art*
        sculptured uncertainty
        no end in sight

I read the artist Hsieh locked himself
in a wooden cage for a year
        another artist lay behind a sheet of glass
        leaning against a wall
until—

so lately, I'm just continuing here
trying to get the details right
        watching leaves fold and fall
        in their own code

        waiting

in this weighty soon-to-be winter air
to find what fits—a hidden hint, a hunch—
        I'm looking closer, listening harder
        under this network of noise

for the smallest stillest farthest whisper

        waiting

for the time taken
to give itself back

STEWING

everything on hand already dumped in the pot
       war with a deadly virus
              wildfires, hurricanes
          knees on necks, guns, guns
yes, plenty of present-day stock—
a bundle of tangled roots stirred in
             race, gender
       politics
          religion
and seared with daily slices
           climate change
              conspiracy theories dredged in lies
           tainted tweets twitters,
add freshly grown and hometown harvested
            ballot babel
          and Russian brine—
curdled butterfat of money
added last, never richer
         for some
               never poorer
         for most
and a blood-red froth rises to the surface
  of this pot of terrible
       stewing
  in my kitchen, on my stove—
        first it boiled
  now it simmers
         low and slow
it smells like forgotten
it tastes like history

OF WHAT I AM NOT

i am not the place
in the middle that knows
how long a good thing will last
or how thick the door
between living and dead
or even the real
name for what is sacred
i am not the leg
gripped by an anklet of current
though i admit to no
fixed notion of up
and down these days
i am not the complaint of old gates
when joy escapes unnoticed
or longhaired animal
appetite rustling in omnivore air
though the world is more
chomped now than i once thought
i am not disaster in the local ditches
or the angel we have yet to hear from
i am not a book still unopened
not the end of a sentence
where another alphabet begins
i am not the person who arrived
or yet the person who will leave
but perhaps i am a cliff
cleaved by the ice
and fire of these jagged times
weathering the hurt

OUT BEYOND BLUE

Much of the world
channels God through blue—
blue-fringed prayer shawl, blue mosque
blue cloak for the handmaid of God
but in Vietnamese, tree leaves and sky are *xanth*—

Color is cagey. Camouflaged in words
our eye glides   slides green to blue
through shades of teal
turquoise, ultramarine.

In the first weeks   babies see
black and white, labels like bright buckets
where successive objects drop.

White: lily-white white knight white collar white hope white Savior
          pure as driven snow

Black: blacklist black mood black mark black sheep black magic
          black-plumed raven *Nevermore*

those sighted slighted buckets fill
white-souled and black-hearted
          binary   subtractive
what we hear colors what we see
what we think we see   holds us hostage
this world half gleam, half cry—

while our eye learns reflection

words wormhole like larvae into our ear
yet doesn't green live inside
the pollen of blue's perception

and standing on the beach
as in after sunset
waves   clouds   sky
all gray
and scented with wild rose.

WHITE PAPER

You caught the messages
in moments of sudden wakening—
of night opening   light streaming
late night news
onto your body of space

your once young son
his mind untangling nets of thought
growing up in this suburban cloister—
its coded meanings— white mama/brown boy.
Ready or not here I come.

You knew there were penalties:
for Driving While Black,
for baggy jeans   fuck you voices
but hadn't he traded these
like his childhood basketball cards

for high school diploma   college ID?
Still, you saw down the color of years
the lack of reliable charts
so you selfied
your white face   paired to his brown

and you transcribed what
streamed from inarticulate darkness
printed out   words and image both
you tucked in the confession booth:
the glove compartment of his sporty black car

to support his story   spilled in the hot light—
this moment
beneath the streetlamp   two cops
knocking on his car window.

He is my son.
This is his car.   NY license...
Words on white paper   your paper-white skin
Are they enough?

still fighting

Woman's March, Sarasota, 2020

hot sun sweet smell
today is
saturday, yes saturday
sometimes my thoughts flutter
sometimes my hands too
like a flock of small birds
in my lap, but not
now
gripping this poster board
the way that osprey I saw
gripped a fish, a whole fish
in his talons
in my fists
a flag and a poster:
1913 and still fighting
even in this wheelchair
still fighting
my mother's yellow pin clipped
to the board
a badge to remind me
nothing snares nothing
she wore it you know
marching for women's right
to vote
the lesson's patience
and passion
now
a smell of dirt
small fires
i followed the rules

i followed them all
now
my ankles are weak
i breathe with this tube in my nose
my voice rasping
through cracked lips of dissent
though a tic of prayer endures
i will not bow my head

TEXT NECK

Sit up straight
my mother said time & again when
she spotted me—moon-shaped arc
angled over book or yellow pad.

What she meant was: skeleton & skin,
our bodies accept habitual placement.
She'd be delighted to find
new evidence, pregnant with implication:

plunked
now in existential twilight glowing
from the shiny faces of tiny screens
butts planted, heads canted forward

kids are growing spikes—

like a horn, a hook,
stalactites at the base of their skulls
just above the neck—penetration
of technology leaving a distinctive sign-off?

John Culkin said *we shape*
our tools & then
our tools shape us.

My mother said
to expect something
from your flesh and senses,
you need to keep your head up.

A GRIMM FAIRY TALE

for my daughter, Jennifer

...Through the leafy woods
      strode Red Riding Hood—
a teacher in this version
   oh, she believed
in forest creatures
      their wings tipped with possibility—
and she believed in rose-colored outcomes
    frogs get kissed,
pumpkins turn to gilded coaches—

Red Riding Hood's basket held no cake
only picture books
    and low tones of nurture
      for the touchy tips
   of small creatures' ears—
and the wolf
    well, he was a young werewolf—
some said he drank from the footprint
   of his father
or slept beneath the marrow of a full moon

but she knew about names
the plague of names sewn onto him like buttons
      bad, lazy, dumb, rebellious, disturbed—
how they accumulate
    weigh a creature down
 like the heavy hide of a wolf—

that October morning

the wolf crouched
             mean—
only a slim wooden desk between
    he curled his lip, he bared his teeth
        raised a knife high above his head—
no woodcutter nearby to save her—
  frightened forest creatures
        cowering beneath her cape—

like some fairy tales
            things don't always end
        happily-ever-after for
trolls, grandmothers, wolves
        even some mermaids and queens
but what of Red Riding Hood—
        there in the chalky woods
      where wolves can be wolves?
  Her wicker basket holds the reasons
        for her still-there
    no grandmother's house in sight

According to the American Psychological Association, one-third of teachers experienced at least one incident of verbal harassment or threat of violence from students during the first full pandemic school year, and 14 percent were physically attacked.

ATOMIC THEORY

August 2020

We humans, boring creatures
monotonously persisting
in just one location.
   Atoms are epic.
   Prone to whimsy.

Encountering Frost's fork
atoms choose
   not the road less traveled
   not the traffic jam—
but both, hedge and verge
in the wooly world
where everything is a wave—
   a world we describe, measure
   but never know.

This world grows weirder—
just this year, a visible star collapsed,
murder hornets turned up near Canada
   not to mention droplets, aerosols
   and every kind of exile

swooping down even now
while I stand stultified
tangled like Gulliver in my own rituals,
   strands of memory: what was not made
   interwoven with strands of what was and is
and cannot be any longer.
Atoms form, orbit, recombine—

whole worlds invent themselves
while I'm mired in concrete dimension
where I never know
if this world is true or
what will happen in the not-now

WRITING MY MEMOIR

Was it the need
to bend, spindle—fold myself over the lives of generations
like the tips of tree roots sending chemicals up the trunk—
an alphabet written in neuron and synapse gauzed
between layers of semantics and syntax
or was it me standing in my constellated past,
breaking myself on a riddle of my own making
or me trying on an old woman's face—
the smell of youth wafting its way through the words?

Perhaps it's true—the way to travel is by story—
sounds bouncing out in strings from the crazy trumpet
of mouth. We keep coming back to—we keep
coming back. Distant memories hold surprises—
sideroads, footpaths—sweet revisions growing underground.
Perhaps those reading it won't fully crack the code,
follow the sprouts growing over my sentences from taproot out
or perhaps they will find me behind a mirror—
a me I never met.

WRITER'S BLOCK

January 2020

Stalled. My gray convolutions suggest coffee.
Then chocolate-covered almonds,
a crumble of Snickerdoodles
spikes the glucose meter
and now I'm prospecting
to find the faults
life cleaves
ice, fire, rain splitting stone
and leaving faint lines to follow—

I take ten—
peel a honeybell orange
fingering for a chord
to make me jump
to make me feel actual
an efflorescence
among the ephemerals.

efflorescence: 1) a flowering out; 4) chemistry:
the migration of a salt to the surface
Followed in the dictionary by
effluence: an emanation—

and then, from the backlit blacklight
in my head—
but isn't writing a poem
just an act of presentation—
poets always mending
or blowing something up?

And yes—

but a poem feeds water to the salts—
I don't know how the chemistry works
but crystals flower in slaptide currents
and in this salty stew
eventually
I hatch
crawl, even swim.

SECOND HAND

I'm a decent enough
craftsperson: I can sand
smooth those sharp pit-holes of syntax

and I've learned to tune
to the higher pitches
circulating in vain attempts—

I've even given up attachment
to sequence

yet I have no imagination
but what I steal

like the pebbles I lift
from the riverbeds
of collective experience.

I thought of this today when I read
the pillars of Stonehenge were likely moved—
an older site dismantled,

hauled 175 miles by migrating tribes
and reassembled, what it used to be
far from where it was.

I admire the craft—revisioning the familiar,
the repositioning, the repolishing of second-hand treasure

but I must admit I want the feel of it—
the sudden sense that comes to a first someone,

that someone with the night mind

looking up at a clot of clouds
or the calligraphy of tree branches
and imagining syntax and metaphor, meaning

we do not yet grasp,
a ring of bluestone
summer solstice shining at the center.

JUMPING TO CONCLUSIONS

I died in Spring, 1967.   Slipped away in other seasons too.
Alight with ripe youth, I died first in Anatomy and Physiology
of laryngotracheal stenosis, etiology idiopathic. Laid-out my
husband   paper-flat against the wall—my hand-printed   hand-
tinted marks on his neck   a disease show-and-tell—his croak
was emphatic   *It's just in the book   you don't have it.*
                    And I might have lived   so neutralized, safe-familiar
except staked like a wager,   a thing I could name: a frosty pillow
of pain beneath my right hip like bone falling from socket
my consternation, not constipation   surely abdominal aortic
aneurysm. He said, *you'll see, it's nothing.*
                              Then somewhere between breast-feeding
and rosebushes   my heart went *thunk kukunk*   clump of four then
a gap rapping against my chest. Cardiovascular disease   eminent
infarction darkened—the woman I dress each day   about to fade
away. *You're fine. I've never been wrong.*
                         And here I should mention   he seems never to tire
of telling what is not   carrying pain from my mind where it
had been   everything. And he returns me each time
like a summering hummingbird noting flowers—
new hours
to my suddenly awaiting life.

FLOWERING BAMBOO

Phyllostachys bambusoides last bloomed in the U.S. in the 1960s

There is no absolute certainty—
this is the way the world works
except when it doesn't.
Even water has no singular posture—
        rippling and embracing
        disquieting, destructive. Maybe
a God
or gods work at exception—
daring us to pare our Absolutes.

At the end of my block, a stand of bamboo—
woody, hollow stalks never budding—
for forty years never tasseling out into flower
but they will—in six or seven decades—
        gregariously—they tell me
with the certainty of time aligned.

Tiny green flowers carrying thousands of seeds
will appear some fumbled afternoon—
        forests of bamboo will burst—bloom in lockstep
in China, Japan, on my own turf.

Hope
in a future is the best I can do:
every stalk of bamboo,
every butterfly, desert pocket mouse,
and me, the pale animal
I ride—
acres of Edens tucked inside.

Notes

"Memoir": after a poem by Joy Kreves.

"The Octopus Escapes" is a tetrahedron pantoum, a poetic form invented by Enriqueta Carrington.

"Text Neck": a growing number of young people have developed a bony external occipital protuberance thought to be a response of the body to smartphone use, a condition dubbed "text neck." Journal of Anatomy, 2016.

Acknowledgments

I am grateful to the editors of the following publications where many of these poems first appeared, sometimes in slightly different versions:

Potomac Review "In Praise of Random Things," "For My Love on his 80th Birthday"
Paterson Literary Review "Phone Home"
Exit 13 "Driving in Portugal"
US 1 Worksheets "Ruby-Red Cherry Woo," "Coming to America," "My Grandson's Zoom Bar Mitzvah," "To My Accent," "Quietude," "Legacy"
Passager "Text Neck,"
Adanna "Every Woman Alive," "Scraped Clean in Istanbul," "Coming to America," "Lilith Goes to Coney Island,"
The New Verse News "Crime Scene," "A Year In,"
Connecticut River Review "Flowering Bamboo,"
Journal of New Jersey Poets "Jumping to Conclusions," "Losing the Ninth," "how is it?" "Out Beyond Blue", "Aftermath," "*that* garden?"
Third Wednesday "Stewing,"
Mount Hope "Inside, Outside, Upside-Down"

"Still She Persisted" appears in the anthology *She Persisted* (Earth's Daughters, 2018)
"White Paper" and "Paper House" appear in the anthology *Show Us Your Papers* (Main Street Rag, 2020)

I wish to thank my critique groups, DVP/US1 Poets' Cooperative and FiveFriendsPoets, who have guided me with skill and kindness. And a particular thank you to my two mentors and dear friends Maxine Susman and Enriqueta Carrington who nurture me and my work with keen and generous spirit.

With gratitude to Ragged Sky Press and to my editor, Ellen Foos, for her careful attention, infinite patience and support. Thanks also to designer Pam Schnitter for her alchemy, spinning manuscript to book. My thanks to Miguel Pagliere for my author photo and the afternoon of laughter and stories shooting it. And always deepest gratitude to my husband, Marty, for holding my hand on this roller-coaster ride.

About the Author

Ilene Millman writes poems about memories, mud, music, making bread, modern times— the array of observation that captures her attention. Her first poetry book, *Adjust Speed to Weather*, was published in 2018. Millman's poems have appeared in print and online journals including, *Nell, Journal of New Jersey Poets, The NewVerse News, Paterson Literary Review, Passager* and *Potomac Review*, and have been included in anthologies such as *She Persists*, and *Forgotten Women*. In 2022 she was nominated for a Pushcart Prize.

Before retiring, Millman worked for more than 35 years as a speech/language therapist teaching children who learn differently. She published two therapy games for elementary and middle school students designed to improve language skills. Millman volunteers for Rock Steady Boxing, an exercise program for people with Parkinson's Disease and does assessment for her county Literacy Volunteers. She lives in Hillsborough, New Jersey.